**RARE WRITING**

# RARE WRITING
## NAPOLEON HILL

A DISTANT MIRROR
Publisher · Bendigo

RARE WRITING
by Napoleon Hill

ISBN-13: 978-1470052683
ISBN-10: 1470052687

Published by A Distant Mirror
*www.adistantmirror.press*
*hello@distantmirror.press*

# Contents

| | |
|---|---|
| Let Ambition be Your Master | 7 |
| What I Have Learned... | 15 |
| How to Sell Your Services | 35 |
| Adversity — A Blessing in Disguise | 53 |
| Self-Control | 59 |
| A Definite Aim in Life | 63 |
| Achievement is Born of Sacrifice | 65 |
| The 17 Principles of Success | 67 |

TEN CENTS PER COPY     JANUARY 1917     $1.00 PER YEAR

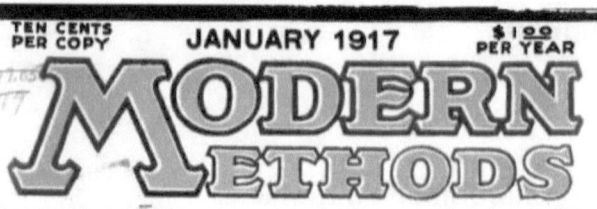

# Modern Methods

## A Monthly Magazine for Business Men

Edited by
*L-E-THURSTON*
DETROIT

Americanism in Industry

Sources of Export Information

Behind the Counter

Letters that Make Customers Stick

# Let Ambition be Your Master

From **Modern Methods**, January 1917.

Lucky is the man who is driven by that determined little slave master called AMBITION! Those who have enjoyed the greatest success in life were literally driven to succeed by AMBITION! It made Harriman, Rockefeller, Carnegie, Hill, Roosevelt and a good many thousands of other successful men of whom we never hear.

Ambition is the mainspring of life, but we must keep it wound up! Self-confidence is the balance wheel which keeps ambition moving at an even momentum. Enthusiasm is the oil with which we keep the human machine greased and in smooth running order. The well organized, capable and productive man is AMBITIOUS, ENTHUSIASTIC, and possesses plenty of SELF-CONFIDENCE. Without these success is uncertain, if not impossible.

One of the greatest men America has ever known divorced his first wife because she was beneath his mental plane, and therefore had a tendency to keep down his ambition. This great man is not with us any more, but the world is testifying to his greatness by quoting his writings and reading his books more than ever before. It is a commonly known fact that his second wife was his chief source of inspiration — that she was responsible for keeping his AMBITION alive and constantly on the alert. That is why he married her. He foresaw the need for a constant attendant who would see to it that his AMBITION let him have no rest.

Lucky is the man who has formed a partnership with such a wife. We all get lazy at times. We need someone to keep our AMBITION alive and spur us on to bigger and better accomplishment. The chief reason that I consent to my wife going back to the farm every summer is that while she is away she constantly writes me letters which fire me with AMBITION. She understands me as few wives understand their husbands. She knows how necessary it is to constantly remind me of my chief aims in life, and she has a way of doing it which is pleasing and inspiring.

When I secured my first $5,000 a year position I thought I was fixed for life, and probably I would have been, had it not been for that little master for whom I was slaving — AMBITION! My wife and AMBITION collaborated against me and made me resign that position — FOR A BIGGER ONE! Five thousand a year would have satisfied me had it not been for my master, AMBITION. In my bigger and broader field I serve a hundred of my fellowmen where I served one before, which means that I get a hundred times as much enjoyment out of life as well as financial returns which are adequate and in proportion to the service which I perform.

In addition to my regular work I lecture three times a week in one of the local colleges, on the subject of Advertising and Salesmanship. The course is a heavy one, covering a period of ten months. The students are taught everything about Advertising and Selling that I can teach them, both from my own experience and from that of a score or more of able advertising specialists. THE FIRST LECTURE IN THE COURSE IS ON THE SUBJECT OF THE VALUE OF AMBITION! I use every ounce of influence that I possess to fire these young men and young women with an everlasting knowledge of the value of AMBITION, SELF-CONFIDENCE and ENTHUSIASM! If I succeed no further than to cause my students to cultivate that wonderful power, AMBITION, my time and their's will have been well spent in the effort.

AMBITION is what freed America from over-the-sea rulership.

Once in my life, while I was working for a salary, I was discharged from my position — just ONCE! The head of the institution for which I worked told me that I was too "ambitious." That was the greatest compliment anyone ever paid me, even though it cut me off temporarily from my bread and meat.

I have always had my suspicions why this man "fired" me, although he claimed it was because his "help" were unanimously agreed that I ought to go! His "help" who objected to me was one of his brothers who had his eye on the general managership of the institution. He knew what "AMBITION" might lead me to. I have never blamed the brother, for he has a wife and two babies to support, and "AMBITION" on my part seemed to him a dangerous barrier between him and his coveted goal.

That institution of which I write was organized nearly twenty years ago. It is doing a business of about $600,000 a year. Another institution, engaged in the same line of business, started in just six years ago, on a capital of less than $6,000. I was formerly Advertising Manager of this institution. It does not discourage "AMBITION." It is now doing a business of $1,500,000 a year, and clearing more net profits every month than the other firm is doing in gross business. The older institution, the one which was organized and has been doing business for nearly twenty years, is headed by men who are afraid of the "AMBITIOUS MAN." Those who are working for a salary are afraid he will get their jobs (which said fear is not without some foundation). The head of the firm is afraid of the "AMBITIOUS MAN" because he is afraid he will find in him a competitor in business (which. also, is not without well grounded foundation).

BUT — AND HERE IS THE CRUX OF MY WHOLE STORY OF THESE TWO FIRMS — THE MAJORITY OF BUSINESS FIRMS ARE LOOKING FOR MEN WHO HAVE PLENTY OF "AMBITION." Do not worry because one firm is afraid of the ambitious man. The very fact that such a firm is afraid of him is, in itself, strong evidence of weakness on the part of those who manage the firm.

While I was Advertising Manager of the younger firm of which I have written, I had three young men in my department. I put them on notice that some day one of them would get my position, and I commenced training them for my job. I told them that the man who "made good" first would get the place, if my recommendations would help any. My Secretary landed the prize. He is still with that firm, making more money than he ever made in his life, and more money than the average man of his age receives. I did not discourage "AMBITION" for fear of losing my job. I encouraged it so that someone would grow to be big enough to push me out of the rut and into a bigger position. That is what happened. I have no patience to speak of, with the man who is so narrow that he is afraid to inspire "AMBITION" in his fellow-workers. Show me a man who believes he has a corner on the details connected with his job and I will show you, in the same person, a man who will never develop beyond petty selfishness.

I beseech you not to fall into the habit of neglecting to cultivate your "AMBITION." You will need something more than mere services with which to succeed. You will need that ever alert little master which is the subject of this chapter. But, I must here give you a word of warning — do not let your ambition become a selfish one! The greatest object over which to develop ambition is the desire to serve our fellowmen. We cannot serve them if we are jealous of them. Remember, also, that AMBITION is a contagious thing. If you give it to the world the world will give it back to you in increased measure. But keep it unto yourself and you will lose it. It will take wings and fly!

Ambition finds expression in a thousand different forms. It is the foundation which underlies all invention, art, music, industry, commerce — nay, the very foundation upon which the progress of the world has been built. Within the present generation we have seen it expressed in the most wonderful inventions the world has ever known; the automobile, the telephone, the wireless, the submarines, the X-ray and the aeroplane. AMBITION was the very warp and woof out of which these things were constructed. Ambition leads us to think, and when we begin to think the nebulous problems in the world's evolution begin to become clarified and simplified.

BE AMBITIOUS IF NOTHING MORE. OTHER THINGS WILL TAKE CARE OF THEMSELVES.

* * *

NAPOLEON HILL

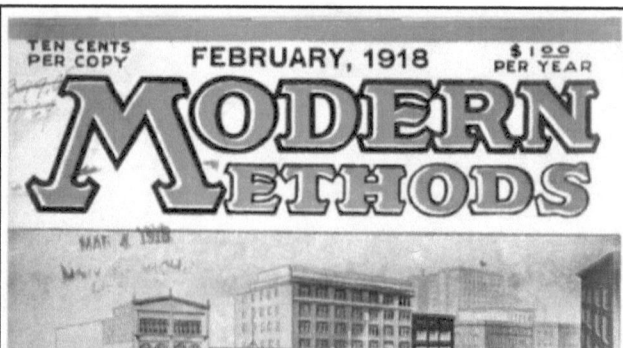

TEN CENTS PER COPY  FEBRUARY, 1918  $1.00 PER YEAR

# MODERN METHODS

## A Monthly Magazine for Business Men

Edited by
*L-E-THURSTON*

DETROIT

Foreign Trade and Your Neighbor

Economy in Deliveries

What Co-Operation Means

Credit Questions and Answers

# What I Have Learned from Analyzing Ten Thousand People

From **Modern Methods**, February 1918.

---

When I was asked to write this article, I was overjoyed at such an opportunity to pass on to thoughtful men and women, who are trying to "find themselves," the benefit of my experience as a personal analyst.

During the past eight years I have analyzed over 10,000 men and women who were earnestly seeking their proper niche in the world's work. Incidentally, through my research I have discovered some of the fundamental qualities without which no human being can hope for success. Five of these are mentioned in this article, in words which a school boy can easily understand.

I have also discovered some of the things which break men's hearts and send them to the scrap-heap of human failures. It is my sincere hope that every person who reads this article may profit by one or more of the points which it covers. I am placing the results of my discoveries in print for the first time, solely out of my deep desire to make life's pathway just a little smoother for my fellow man.

It is my purpose to pass on to you, in as few words as possible, that portion of my discoveries which I believe will aid you in planning and achieving your 'chief aim' in life, whatever that may be. I shall not preach to you. Whatever suggestions I make are based upon discoveries which I have made in my work.

I believe it befitting to state that twenty years ago I was working as a laborer, at wages of $1 a day. I had no home and no friends. I had but little education. My future then looked very unpromising. I was downcast in spirit. I had no ambition. I had no definite purpose in life. All around me I saw men, some young and some old, who were whipped — just as I felt that I was. I absorbed my environment as a sponge absorbs water. I became a part of the daily routine in which I lived.

It had never occurred to me that I could ever amount to anything. I believed my lot in life was to be that of a laborer. I was just like a horse which has had the bit slipped into its mouth and the saddle buckled on its back.

Here is the turning point in my career. Note it well!

A chance remark, no doubt made in a half-jocular way, caused me to throw the bit out of my mouth, kick off the saddle and 'run away' as young horses sometimes do. That remark was made by a farmer with whom I lived. I shall never forget it if I live to be a hundred, because it has partly bridged the gap over that awful chasm which nearly all human beings want to cross — 'failure'!

The remark was this: "You are a bright boy. What a pity you are not in school instead of at work as a laborer at a dollar a day."

"You are a bright boy!" These were the sweetest words I had ever heard.

That remark aroused in me the first ambition I had ever felt, and, incidentally, it is directly responsible for the Personal Analysis system which I have worked out. No one had ever hinted to me before that I was '"bright." I had always imagined that I was exceedingly dull. In fact, I had been told that I was a dunce. As a boy I was defeated in everything I undertook, largely because those with whom I associated ridiculed me and discouraged me from engaging in the things which interested me most. My work was selected for me — my associates were selected for me — my studies were selected for me — and my play, well, I was,taught that play was a waste of time.

With this first-hand knowledge of the great handicap under which the average person starts out in life, as a working basis, I began many years ago to work out a system for helping people "find themselves" as early in life as possible. My efforts have yielded splendid returns for I have helped many find the work for which they were most suited, and started them on the road to happiness and success. I have helped not a few to acquire the qualities for success which are mentioned in this article.

## The First Two Success Requisites

With this prelude I shall tell you first what I believe to be the two most important of the five chief requisites for success. These are SELF-CONFIDENCE and ENTHUSIASM. The other three

I will mention later.

What is self-confidence?

I will tell you what it is: It is the little glass window through which you may look and see the real man-power within your body. Self-confidence is self-discovery — finding out who you are and what you can do. It is the banishment of fear. It is the acquirement of mental courage. It is the turning on of the light of human intelligence, through the use of common sense.

It was self-confidence, plus enthusiasm and concentration, that caused the birth of the world's greatest inventions, the incandescent electric light, the automobile, the talking machine, the aeroplane, the moving picture and all the other great mechanical creations.

Self-confidence, then, is an essential quality for all worth-while accomplishments. Yet, it is the quality in which most of us are weakest. Not a weakness which many of us acknowledge, but it exists just the same. A man without self-confidence is like a ship without a rudder — he wastes his energy without moving in the right direction.

I wish I might be able to tell you exactly how to acquire full self-confidence. That would be a big undertaking. I will give you this suggestion, however — I made my first step in the direction of self-confidence the day I heard those words, "You are a bright boy." That was the first time I had ever felt ambition tugging at my coat sleeve, and with it, apparently, came self-confidence.

It is remarkable what clothes have to do with' building self-confidence. A man came to me for analysis not long ago. He had been earning a good salary, but conditions for which he was in no way responsible caused him to be let out. I asked him how much money he had and he said, "Seventy-five dollars." I told him to invest one-third of it in a new suit of clothes. He demurred on the ground that he "couldn't afford it." But I insisted and went with him to buy the clothes. Then I insisted on his going to the cobbler's and having the heels of his shoes straightened up. Then I persuaded him to have his shoes shined and get a clean shave and a hair cut. I then sent him to see the president of a large corporation who employed him at $3,000 a year.

If I had sent him to interview the president of that 'corporation without the new suit and the clean-up, he wouldn't have gotten the position, in all probability, because he would not have had the proper self-confidence. Good clothes, clean linen, polished shoes and a clean shave are not luxuries — they are a necessity to the man who comes in contact with the business public.

## The Second Success Requisite

Then comes the second requisite for success, enthusiasm, that great dynamic force which puts self-confidence into action. Enthusiasm may be likened to the steam which runs the locomotive. The most powerful locomotive ever built might stand upon the side-track with coal in the bunker and the engineer in the cab, but if there is no steam the wheels will not turn — there is no action.

It is exactly the same with the human machine. If there is no enthusiasm there is little or no action. Lack of these qualities — self-confidence and enthusiasm — stands between the great majority of men and success. This statement is no mere conjecture upon my part. I have proved it in thousands of cases. I am proving it in more than a hundred cases a week right along. Enthusiasm is something which cannot be counterfeited. Only the real article will fill the bill. Enthusiasm usually comes automatically when you find the vocation into which you can pitch your whole heart and soul — the work you love best.

## The Third Success Requisite

The third requisite for success is a definite working plan — the habit of working with a "chief aim" in life. From my work as a vocational director I have learned that most people have no such plan. Men who are working without a well defined plan — without a pre-determined objective — are going nowhere in particular and most of them are getting nowhere. In my personal analysis chart, which all whom I examine must fill out, is this question:

"What is your chief aim in life?"

An actual tabulation of answers to this question shows that only one out of every fifty has any "chief aim." But few have any sort of a real aim, "chief" or otherwise. Yet, nearly all whom I have analyzed expect to succeed. Just when, or how. or in what work the majority of them do not undertake to say.

Nearly every man wants a "big position," yet not one out of a hundred, even though he may be competent, knows how to get it. A "big position" is not something that we find hanging on a bush ready to be plucked off by "pull" by the first person who comes along. It is the sum total of a number of smaller positions or tasks which we have efficiently filled; not necessarily with different firms, but, as often as otherwise, in the employment of one firm. A big position is built just as we build a big sky-scraper — by first formulating a definite plan and then building according to that plan, step by step.

The possible exception to this rule is the man who gets into a "big position" through "pull." There are exceptions to most rules, but the question to ask yourself is this:

"Am I willing to go through life and take a chance on getting ahead on 'pull'?"

Look about you and I dare say you will find that for every man who is succeeding by "pull" you may find a hundred who are succeeding by "push"!

There are varying degrees of success, just as there are different ideas as to what success is, but whether your idea of success is the accumulation of wealth or the rendering of some great service to mankind, or both, you will not likely achieve it unless you have a "chief aim" — a definite goal with a definite plan mapped out for reaching it.

No architect ever started a building until he had first created a perfect picture of it in his mind, and then carefully transferred the detail of the picture to a blue-print! And no human being may hope to build a worthwhile success until he has planned the building and decided what it shall be.

## Selecting a Vocation

A very large proportion of the people whom I have analyzed are in positions which they hold, not by selection, but by chance. Even those who are following vocations which they deliberately chose, in the majority of cases, have not observed even the most elementary rules of self-analysis. They have never stopped to find out whether or not the work in which they are engaged is the work for which they are best fitted by nature and education.

For example, a young man whom I recently analyzed, had prepared himself for the practice of law, but had made an utter failure of that profession. He failed, first, because he did not like the profession after he got into it; secondly, because he had absolutely no native ability for that profession. He was badly deformed physically and, as a consequence, made a very poor impression before courts and juries. He lacked enthusiasm and that dynamic force which we call "personality," without which he could not hope to succeed as a lawyer. Such a person might succeed to some extent as advisory counsel or "office lawyer," but not as a trial lawyer where a strong personality and the ability to speak with force and conviction count for so much.

The surprising part of this particular case was the fact that this man had never understood just why he did not succeed in the practice of law. It seemed simple enough to him after I had pointed out the negative qualities which I believed had stood between him and success. When I asked him how he came to take up law, he replied. "Well, I just had a hunch that I would like it!"

## "I just had a hunch that I would like it!"

Selecting a life work on a "hunch" is a dangerous thing. You wouldn't purchase a race-horse on a "hunch"; you would want to see him perform on the track. You wouldn't purchase a bird-dog on a "hunch"; you would want to see him in action or know something of his pedigree. If you selected a bird-dog in this haphazard way, you might find yourself trying to set birds with a bull-pup!

A court reporter, whom I analyzed, said to me: "My fifteen years of experience have proved to me that a jury seldom tries the defendant, but instead, they try the lawyers in the case. The lawyer who makes the best impression generally wins." Everyone who is familiar with court actions knows that this is too often true. You can see, therefore, what an important part "personality" plays in the practice of law.

Mr. Carnegie says that his success is due largely to his ability to pick men. Mr. Frank A. Vanderlip and Mr. Rockefeller say the same. If you will stop and analyze all the successful men you know, you will probably find that they either possess all the requisites for success in the business in which they are engaged, or, they know how to select men who will supply what they lack — men who are their opposites in nearly every particular.

Probably fifty per cent of those who call themselves salesmen are of poor personal appearance, have weak faces, and speak without force. A salesman conveys to his prospective buyer a positive or negative influence, according to his own,personality and manner of approach in presenting his case. A man who is badly deformed, or the man who suffers from impediment of speech and otherwise makes a negative appearance had better not take up oral salesmanship. If he can hide behind the written page, he may succeed, but in person never!

## The Fourth Success Requisite

The fourth success requisite is the habit of performing more service than you are actually paid for. It is the practice of the majority of men to perform no more service than they feel they are being paid to perform. Fully eighty per cent of all whom I have analyzed were suffering on account of this great mistake.

You need have no fear of competition from the man who says, "I'm not paid to do that, therefore I'll not do it." He will never be a dangerous competitor for your job, but watch out for the fellow who does not let his pick hang in the air when the whistle blows, or the man who stays at his desk or work bench until his work is finished — watch out that such a fellow does not "Challenge you at the post and pass you at the grandstand," as Andrew Carnegie said.

Before mentioning the fifth and last requisite for success I shall ask your indulgence while I digress for just a few moments. After I had commenced work on this article I decided to have the five points which I have covered put to the acid test to see whether or not they would square up with the experience of other vocational directors. I took the manuscript to Dr. J. M. Fitzgerald, Chicago, who is, without doubt, the most able vocational director in the world.

Dr. Fitzgerald went over the manuscript with me word for word and I have his permission to quote him as saying that he fully endorses the five chief points covered by this article. He says that they square up with his own experience, exactly.

But, before we went over the manuscript, I asked Dr. Fitzgerald to state the chief negative qualities which he had discovered to be standing as barriers between those whom he had analyzed and success. His reply was quick and concise, as follows:

1) Lack of self-discernment; the lack of ability upon part of most men to analyze themselves and find the work for which they are best prepared.

2) Lack of intensified concentration and the disposition not to put more into their work than they expect to get out of it.

3) Lack of moral self-control.

Dr. Fitzgerald has analyzed, in person, more than 15,000 men and women. Many of the largest corporations of the middle West will not employ a man for any important position until he has been analyzed by Dr. Fitzgerald. He has taken men from the bookkeeper's desk and enabled them to become successful executives. He has converted clerks into managers in much less time than is ordinarily required, merely by having started them in the right direction, through accurate personal analysis.

I mention these details concerning Dr. Fitzgerald's work because I want you to feel that my own experience, as stated in this article, is not mere conjecture on my part — that it is authentic and that it has the endorsement of the world's greatest personal analyst. Bear in mind that the five chief points covered by this article have been discovered, classified and charted from the personal analysis of 25,000 people, 10,000 of whom I have analyzed and 15,000 of whom were analyzed by Dr. Fitzgerald.

## The Fifth Success Requisite

This article ought to be of benefit to those who are about to select a vocation and those who are in the wrong vocation but wish to make a change. However, there is another class to be taken into consideration. It is represented by those who have selected the right vocation but who, nevertheless, are not succeeding. I have found the Key to Success for this class. In this Great Magic Key you will find the fifth and last of the success rules which I have discovered in my vocational work.

In presenting to you this key let me first explain that it is no invention of mine.

This great 'Magic Key' is a most wonderful power, yet perfectly simple of operation. So simple that most people have failed to make use of it. We human beings are too prone to look askance at so simple a formula for success — a formula which will open the door to health and wealth; yet, such a formula is the Great Magic Key.

Through the Great Magic Key we have unlocked the secret doors to all of the world's great inventions. Through its magic powers all of our great geniuses have been produced.

We will suppose that you desire a better position. The Great Magic Key will help you attain it! Through its use Carnegie, Rockefeller, Hill, Harriman, Morgan and Guggenheim have accumulated millions of dollars in material wealth.

You ask "What is this Great Magic Key?"

And I answer with one word: *concentration*!

To stop here would be insufficient. You must know how to use this Great Magic Key! First, let me tell you that *ambition* and *desire* are the great dynamic powers which you must summon to the aid of *concentration*. They form the lock which this great key fits. Without ambition and desire the Great Magic Key is useless. The reason that so few people use the key is that most people lack ambition!

Desire whatever you may, and if your desire is strong enough the Great Magic Key of *concentration* will help you attain it, if the object of your desire is something which it is humanly possible for you to attain.

There are learned men of science who tell us that the wonderful powers of prayer itself operate through the principle of *concentration*, plus faith and strong *desire*!

I am making no attempt to associate the Great Magic Key with occultism or religion. I am treating it from the ordinary layman's viewpoint. I am dealing with it from actual knowledge that I have gained in carefully analyzing and charting over 10,000 people.

We will assume that you are skeptical of the powers of *concentration* and *desire*. Let's put these powers to the test, through a concrete example, for unless we do this it would be just like telling you to be honest without telling you how to be honest.

## How to Concentrate

First, you must do away with skepticism and doubt! No unbeliever ever enjoyed the benefits of these great powers. You must believe in the test which I am going to ask you to make. You must let no feeling of unbelief creep in.

Now we will suppose that you have thought of becoming a great writer, or a great public speaker, or a great business executive, or a great advertising manager. Suppose we take the latter as the subject of this test. But remember that if you expect results you must follow instructions to the letter.

Take a plain piece of paper, ordinary letter size, and write on it in large letters — the largest it will carry — these words:

> *I am going to become a successful advertising manager because this will enable me to render the world a useful service — and because it will provide me with the necessary material things of life!*
>
> *I will concentrate on this desire for ten minutes daily, just before retiring and just after rising.*
>
> *(Sign your name.)*

If you are not good at lettering just clip out the foregoing, sign it, and place where you will read it just before retiring and just after getting up each day. Do exactly as you have pledged yourself to do, for at least ten days.

Now when you come to do your "CONCENTRATING" this is the way to go about it:

Look ahead three, five, ten, or even fifteen years from now and see yourself in a position as advertising manager paying a big salary. See the happy faces of your loved ones — maybe a wife and babies — maybe a mother .with silvery hair. Be a dreamer if you choose to call it that, but be also a "doer"! The world needs this combination of "dreamer-doers." They are the Lincolns, Grants, Edisons, Hills, Carnegies, Vanderlips and Schwabs.

See yourself laying aside a "nest-egg" for a rainy day. See yourself in your motor car which you will be able to afford. See yourself in your own cozy little home that you will own.

See yourself a person of influence in the business world. See yourself INCREASING IN VALUE AND EARNING STILL MORE MONEY as you grow older. See yourself engaged in a line of work where you will not fear the loss of a job when the gray hairs begin to put in their appearance.

Paint this picture through the powers of your imagination, and lo! it will turn into Desire. Use this Desire as the chief object of your CONCENTRATION, and see what happens!

It may take longer than ten days for you to master this lesson in concentration. Again it may take only one day. That will depend upon how well you perform the task.

You now have the secret of the Great Magic Key!

It will unlock the door to whatever position in life you want, if that position is one that you are prepared by nature and education to fill. It will make of you a better citizen and show you the road to true happiness if the object of your concentration is a worthy one.

Use this Great Key with intelligence! Use it only for the attainment of worthy purposes, and it will give you the things of life for which your heart may crave. So simple, so easy of application, yet so MARVELOUS IN RESULTS! Try it! Begin right now. Forget the mistakes you have made in the past. Start all over again, and make the next five or ten years tell a story of human accomplishment in whatever line of work your calling may have placed you, that you will not be ashamed of — that the future generations of your family will be PROUD OF!

MAKE A NAME FOR YOURSELF THROUGH AMBITION, DESIRE AND CONCENTRATION!

Vocational guidance has not yet become a universally accepted science. It may never be accepted as a science by everyone, but this does not preclude a person from using common sense in selecting a vocation. The trouble is, too many people act on a "hunch." If you are engaged in work in which you are not succeeding, take inventory of yourself and see if you cannot locate the trouble. The chances are that you can. Just apply common sense in selecting a life work. You may not be able to analyze yourself as well as a man who has many years of experience could do, therefore, if you have any doubts place yourself in the hands of a man who is experienced in analyzing men. He will undoubtedly see your weak spots more quickly than you could. Few of us can be our own best critics because we are inclined to overlook our weaknesses or place too little importance on them.

There are but few, if any, ironclad rules to follow in the selection of a vocation that would apply in every case. Probably these come as near being applicable in all cases as is possible: Be sure you love the vocation you adopt. Be sure you are enthusiastic over it and that you intend to stick to it. Be sure you are prepared, educationally, for the work you select. Be sure the vocation is one in which you can render a service that is beneficial to humanity. Be sure the work is permanent. Be sure that it is work that will not impair your health.

Let me summarize the five chief requisites for success, so you will not forget them. They are —

1) Self-confidence;

2) Enthusiasm;

3) Working with a 'chief aim';

4) Performing more work than you are paid for;

5) Concentration, backed by desire and unwavering faith.

By a reasonably intelligent application of these qualities you can become master of your own career.

Finally, I wish to leave this thought with you. It has been my constant companion through life. It has supported my tired legs when they would otherwise have allowed me to fall by the wayside.

It is this:

"Every adversity is, in reality, a blessing in disguise. The university of hard knocks sends forth its graduates to fight life's battles, with plenty of strength to overcome every obstacle that may confront them. From every failure we may learn a great lesson if we will. Somewhere in the world your place is waiting for you. Through persistence and intelligent effort you will eventually find it. You will never be defeated in your life's purpose if you keep faith in the only person in the world who controls your destiny — yourself!"

* * *

# Modern Methods
## A BUSINESS MAN'S MAGAZINE

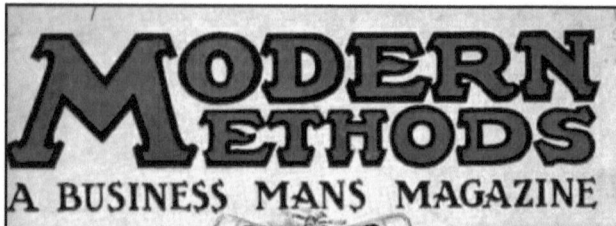

Edited by
L. E. THURSTON
Detroit

**The Government's Foreign Trade Service**
By Burwell S. Cutler, Chief of the Bureau of Foreign and Domestic Commerce

**What to Look for in a Partner**

**The Morale of Our Army in Overalls**

**Uncle Sam, Storekeeper**

TEN CENTS A COPY        JULY, 1918

# How To Sell Your Services

From **Modern Methods**, June-July 1918.

---

Before we start, may I not remind you that we intend to go much farther than the mere question of telling you "how to get a job"? We are going with you to the very bottom of this subject and we shall uncover the chief fundamental principles through which you may not only get "a" job, but through which you may get "the" job for which you are best suited!

We shall go still deeper into this world-wide-important subject and show you how to fill the position satisfactorily and profitably after you get it!

The great gateway to fame and fortune through which all who succeed must pass might properly be labeled "Personal Service!" All that you have or ever will have to give in return for the fortune which you hope to accumulate is personal services!

Ponder over this and you will unconsciously lay the foundation for the point which I wish to make, namely, that the size of that fortune will depend, not upon what you wish it to be, but upon the quality and quantity of service you render the world!

It would be impossible to give you a definite rule to follow that would apply in all cases, but you may put it down as an essential requirement that success will never crown your efforts in any undertaking unless you please the purchaser of your services. Your services may be satisfactory in both quality and quantity, but this is not enough — your method of rendering your services must actually please the purchaser!

I am writing almost within the shadow of one of the largest and best known retail merchandise establishments in the world — Marshall Field & Company. That great business was built upon just one simple idea, and that idea was this: "That every customer must go away from the store "satisfied." Profits are secondary when it comes to delivering with the goods sold at Marshall Field's, service that actually pleases the buyer and makes him or her want to come back again.

A short time ago I had lunch with Mr. McKinley, Vice-President of Marshall Field & Company. He said that one of the biggest problems confronting them was that of training their employees to reflect this spirit of service in every transaction, large or small. Marshall Field saw clearly, without anyone to suggest it to him, the commercial value of pleasing the buyer, yet the big task in keeping Marshall Field alive in those who now manage the Field store is to get the 3,000 employees to absorb a relatively small proportion of the Field idea of service!

I do not presume to be able to tell you how to please those whom you serve and to whom you are selling your services, but I do tell you to seek until you find the right method and then make use of it!

Marshall Field's problem was exactly the same as yours — to market personal services along with his merchandise so there would be satisfaction and repeat orders. Nothing could be more simple than this.

It is an interesting experience and a rare privilege to study the officials of the Marshall Field Store at close range. In these men you may find one principle in common which we could all well afford to copy, and that is the principle of "service."

Herein, then, is the secret of the success of the Field business, even though the founder has been dead many years. The principle of service, if rightly administered, never dies! Through application of this principle you may bury yourself in the hearts of your fellowmen, where the principles for which you stand will live long after your body has gone back to dust.

You will succeed only by selling satisfactory service — by pleasing those who purchase your services! Keep this ever in mind and the road-way of satisfactory service will open to you when you need it!

If I have seemed to dwell at length on this prelude on "Service," may it not be possible that I am justified by the importance of the subject?

This brings us to a suitable point at which to present a complete chart of the chief factors which enter into the sale of personal services of every nature whatsoever. Our intention is to make this chart so thorough and yet so simple that anyone may make immediate application of it.

The first factor for consideration is the selection of the right position, in a line of work for which you are best fitted by nature, training, inclination and experience.

The method through which to select the "right" position is one which cannot be fully explained, for lack of sufficient space. All else being equal, however, the position you select should be the one which YOU LIKE BEST! From this point on we shall go on the assumption that you have selected the RIGHT vocation — that you have had vocational counsel through which you have properly determined this question.

The following is a complete analysis chart which covers all of the important subjects connected with the sale of personal services:

**1) Analysis of your product**

Under this heading, before you proceed to offer your services for sale, you will take inventory, so to speak, to arrive at the following facts as a basis for offering your services:

a) What sort of services have you to market?

b) Value of the services you have to offer.

c) Who is the most available purchaser?

You will not have even a starting point until you have accurately organized this information.

**2) The service you render**

a) Quality must be right.

b) Quantity must be right.

c) Your method of rendering it must be satisfactory to the purchaser.

## 3) Cause and effect

a) The service you render is CAUSE.

b) The pay you receive is EFFECT.

If the "effect" is not satisfactory examine "cause" and you will find the reason.

## 4) Opportunity to display a sample of your 'goods'

Getting a job is a mere preliminary or chance to show a small sample of the sort of service you can render. As we shall show you later on, the actual procuring of the job is of only secondary importance.

## 5) Methods of securing position

a) By application in person.

b) Application by letter.

c) Advertisement in newspapers.

d) Application through employment agencies.

e) Attracting employers to you through unusually satisfactory services rendered.

As you will see later on, if you offer your services by applying in person it will be necessary for you to carefully guard your personal appearance. If you apply by letter it will be necessary for you to properly construct that letter and guard its "personal appearance" as carefully as you would your own if you were applying in person.

## 6) Gathering and organizing data concerning a position and the firm or individual for whom you wish to work

By this is meant the gathering of all available facts concerning 'the position you wish to secure, and all information concerning the firm or individual with whom you wish to work, the nature of the business, and particularly all data that would be of benefit to you in creating a sales argument that would show you to be fully qualified to fill the position before you actually apply for it. All of this data should be fully assimilated, organized and correlated, thereby preparing yourself to show just where and how you would fit into the position that you seek.

## 7) Qualities that will make your services desirable and even sought by employers

a) Willingness on your part — not only a "willingness" but an intense desire — to perform more work than you are paid for.

b) Intense interest and boundless enthusiasm in your work.

c) Pleasing personality: cheerfulness, optimism, courage.

d) Self-confidence.

e) Initiative: habit of seeing and actually performing more work than the job you fill requires, without being told to do so.

f) Action: habit of doing your work promptly.

g) Power of Analysis: ability to see more, hear more and know more about your job and the business of the concern for which you work than those around you. Ability to gather, organize, classify and correlate all RELEVANT facts concerning every task you perform and every responsibility that you assume.

h) Willingness to and actual practice of reaching outside of the immediate sphere of your own duties and assuming more responsibilities.

i) Leadership — the ability to get others to perform work willingly and gladly, with cheerfulness, not merely because they are afraid not to do so, but because they wish to do so. The ability to command the respect and confidence of associate workers, whether in a higher or lower position.

j) Loyalty — as a matter of course.

k) Persistence — not only the ability but the actual practice of properly finishing all that you start.

l) Concentration — the ability to keep your mind focused on a task until it has been completed.

Now, let us give you a few brief suggestions as to the proper use of the foregoing chart. Probably the most satisfactory method to follow is this: Write your name at the top of a sheet of paper and analyze your "product" — the services you wish to market — under the heading of "(1) ANALYSIS OF YOUR PRODUCT." Write out a complete description of the sort of services you have to market, what you believe the value of these services to be, and a list of names of the most available and desirable employers, if you have ascertained them.

This will give you a splendid starting point, and everything must have a beginning.

Under the heading of "(2) SERVICE YOU RENDER" you should write out a complete description of what you believe to be the QUALITY of your services, the QUANTITY you intend to deliver to the prospective employer, and the method or "spirit" in which you intend to deliver this service.

Under the heading of "(3) CAUSE AND EFFECT" you should write out, in your own words, your understanding of the principle that "the service you render is CAUSE, while the pay you receive is EFFECT." This is a principle which you will do well to thoroughly understand and apply.

There is a cause for every effect!

Is it not reasonable, therefore, to suppose that there is a CAUSE for unsatisfactory remuneration for personal services rendered? The cause may be traceable to the person who renders the services, or it may be traced to the purchaser, who in some instances is selfish and unfair. In the majority of cases, however, you will find the cause connected with one or all of the following:

1) The quality of services rendered unsatisfactory.

2) The quantity of services rendered unsatisfactory.

3) The manner in which services are rendered unsatisfactory.

If you find the trouble here you will readily see that it is one which only the seller can eliminate.

Before blaming the purchaser of your services with your lean pay envelope it is well to analyze yourself by applying this formula and ascertaining whether or not you are at fault. If you are not at fault — if the quality of your services is A-1, the quantity is abundant and the manner in which you are rendering the service highly satisfactory — and still the pay envelope is not sufficient, there are only two conclusions at which to arrive:

Either you are a poor salesman, or the purchaser of your services is unjust and unfair.

If your salesmanship is poor you can improve it and if the purchaser of your services is unjust or shortsighted and unfair with you. find another purchaser!

Failure to comply with one or the other of these suggestions is the chief reason why men and women of ability go through life, chained to mediocre positions, failures!

Under the heading "(4) OPPORTUNITY TO DISPLAY YOUR 'GOODS'" you should write out your understanding, in your own words, that a job is nothing more than a beginning point — a chance to "deliver the goods," so to speak. The biggest job in the world is nothing more than a mere "chance" to sell your services as long as you please your purchaser.

The reason so few people have big jobs is due very largely to the fact that so few people regard their jobs in the nature of an "opportunity." Nearly every job is a "big job" in the "making."' Nearly every job has the potentialities of a big job, if properly developed.

Under the heading of "(5) METHODS OF SECURING POSITION" you should write down all of the available channels through which you intend to seek employment, unless, of course, you merely wish to market your services to better advantage with your present employer, which is often the best thing to do.

If you apply in person you should be careful of your personal appearance. This applies to the person seeking a position as bricklayer as much as it does to the person seeking an executive or clerical position in an office. Slovenliness and an unsightly appearance always carry a negative effect that makes it hard for such a person to sell his or her services to best advantage. In many positions no one would even be considered who did not have a prepossessing, well kept personal appearance.

If there is ever a time when you should look your "best" it is when you go to interview the person to whom you hope to sell your services to best advantage. This is true not alone because of the favorable impression which it will create in the purchaser's mind, but also because of the additional courage and self-confidence which it will give YOU! Clean and well pressed clothes, clean linen, carefully brushed hair, clean finger nails and a quick, re-assuring, springy step which goes with these things, is an asset that you will need; nay, an asset that you cannot afford lo be without!

In offering your services by letter you should be sure to send out your little personal messenger dressed in the best of "clothes" — stationery! The first appearance of your letter may determine its fate, just as the first glance at a person who applies in person may determine his fate.

Of course good stationery alone will not turn the trick. It merely secures for your letter first attention. In "How to Sell Your Services" (which you can purchase from "Modern Methods") you will find specimen letters and detailed information as to the proper way to write the actual contents of the letter itself. Space will not permit us to take up this subject at this time.

Personally, if I were applying for a position I would prefer to make use of both the letter and personal interview. I would select my prospective employer, and through one or more carefully written letters I would endeavor to make him feel that he wanted to see me in person. I would avoid, if possible, bringing him to a point where he could say "no" before he had seen me in person. The purpose of the letter or letters would be entirely to make the prospective employer feel that he wanted to talk to me. I would so construct my letters that he would request me to come and see him.

A good way to begin such a campaign would be to first gather all of the information and facts available concerning the prospective employer's business in general, and the position that you desired to fill, in particular!

I would not say a word about a position, but instead I would go right ahead and submit some concrete suggestions that he could make use of in connection with his business, whether he employed me or not. In other words, I would actually attach myself to his working staff, without pay, and without asking his permission. This (unusual) procedure would be sure to gain "favorable attention" for me and from this point on negotiations would be easy!

The last mentioned method of "attracting employers to you through unusually satisfactory services rendered" needs but little comment. While this method has been mentioned last, it is nevertheless the most important of all those mentioned, to all except those who are applying for their first position. This for the reason, as we have already stated, that in every position there are undeveloped possibilities that one may develop by rendering the right sort of service.

Lucky is the person who looks upon his position as an "opportunity to attract favorable attention because he is rendering unusually satisfactory service!" Such a person is bound to succeed; if not in his present position, then in a bigger and better one somewhere else.

No lawyer of reputation would think of going into court with a case until he had gathered every available fact and every scintilla of information concerning it. He would organize these facts and be prepared to present them to the court in logical sequence.

You must be prepared to do the same when you present yourself for employment.

This brings us to the last subject, "(7) CAUSES THAT WILL MAKE YOUR SERVICES DESIRABLE — EVEN SOUGHT BY EMPLOYERS." No argument need be advanced to prove that all the qualities mentioned under the above heading, in the foregoing chart, are desirable ones to develop, but the question is, how may these qualities be developed in a person who does not already possess them?

Before answering this question it will be necessary to briefly mention a principle through the operation of which all of these qualities and others as well may be quickly developed. I have reference to AUTO-SUGGESTION.

Auto-suggestion, as you of course know, means simply self-suggestion or suggestion that we make to ourselves. It is surprising, however, to know how few people actually understand the possibilities of achievement through the use of auto-suggestion. It it not my intention to enter into any lengthy argument as to the merits of auto-suggestion. I know that it has worked wonders in my own life and I have seen it work wonders in the lives of others — wonders which, in many respects, seemed as miraculous as anything that happened in the Biblical days of two thousand years ago!

In digressing from the subject of "How To Sell Your Services," to briefly discuss the method through which you may develop those desirable positive qualities, I am taking it for granted that you wish to be thorough — that you want all the available information you can get, not only on the secondary question of securing an immediate job, but also on the more important subject of ascertaining how to build that job into a bigger and more profitable one.

To give you this information I must at least discuss briefly the subject of auto-suggestion, for it will be through application of this principle that you will cultivate the qualities necessary in filling a big position.

It has been proved by the world's most able scientists and psychologists that every thought or idea placed in the human mind and systematically held there, through concentration, has a tendency to reproduce itself after its kind, in bodily, muscular action. For example, if you think of fear constantly you will be afraid and your bodily actions will be directed accordingly. On the other hand, if you think courage your bodily actions will be courageous. If you hate another person that person will likely hate you, because you cannot think hate and keep from showing it in one way or another, through bodily action, facial expression, etc.

The greatest of all philosophers and teachers probably had in mind the principle of auto-suggestion when he said:

"Whatsoever ye soweth that shall ye also reap!"

If you will take my word for it I will assure you that I have experimented with this principle until I know that it is as immutable as is the law of gravitation.

"Is it possible," I hear you say, "that by simply placing in my mind the thoughts which I would like to see reproduced in physical reality, I can accomplish such remarkable results?"

And I answer, "not only is this possible, but it is unavoidable!"

This being true you can readily see how important it is to make use of the principle of auto-suggestion. The procedure is very simple. Probably that is why so few people have had enough faith in it to make a more organized application of it.

Let us make use of this principle in developing the foregoing list of desirable qualities, from "a" to "l." Take the first one, for example, number it 1 and write out the following sentence:

1 — From this day on I will cheerfully perform more work than I am paid to perform, never complaining, because I know that in time this habit will be appreciated by my employers and I will be paid accordingly.

One of the remarkable things about auto-suggestion is the fact that the very minute you write out this sentence, (if you sincerely intend to do what you have pledged) you will find your every action directed toward carrying out your pledge!

Then, take the next quality that you desire to develop, and write it out as follows:

2 — I love my work and from this day on I will be ever alert for opportunities to do better work and more of it. I am enthusiastic over and intensely interested in my work and I will do everything in my power to perform it more satisfactorily than any other person could.

Go right down the list until you have written out every quality which you intend to develop, in every case stating, in your own words, just what you are going to do to develop that quality. When the list is complete commit it to memory by reading it aloud several times a day. Auto-suggestion is most effective when it is followed by action as well as mere affirmations or wishes. The mere words which you use are not so important as long as they represent definite positive ideas or thoughts. Your affirmations must not be vague, however, because if they are the results will also be vague.

This is all there is to the principle of auto-suggestion; at least all that I can tell you about. If you do not make application of the principle it will not benefit you. It works no miracles without your hearty and persistent co-operation! But, with these, it will give you the surprise of your life and place you wherever you wish to be among men!

\* \* \*

# THE SQUARE DEAL

Current Discussions of Industrial Problems

**Domestic Industrial News
Foreign Industrial Notes
Things Worth Knowing
Current Business Discussions
Human Betterments
Editorial Comment
Poetry - Fiction - Humor**

Published Monthly by
The Square Deal Press, Ltd.
Battle Creek, Mich.

AUGUST
SEPTEMBER 1915

$1.00 A YEAR
10c A COPY

VOLUME XVII

NUMBER CXXI

# ADVERSITY;
# A BLESSING IN DISGUISE

From **The Square Deal**, Aug-Sept, 1915

Friend, do not become discouraged, disappointed and disheartened, if the seemingly cruel hand of fate knocks you off of your feet. Maybe the blow will prove to be the greatest blessing that ever came your way.

It has happened to many and doubtless it will happen to you, when the dark clouds of despair have darkened the pathway of life's progress, that behind each dark cloud is a silver lining, if we only learn how to see it.

There were two men who established and built up an enormously successful commercial institution. They owned the stock in the company about equally. One of the men, who had lots of initiative, began selling off some of his stock, thus enjoying for personal use a large amount of ready cash from the proceeds.

His associate in the business, who didn't possess quite so much initiative, wanted to sell some of his personal stock that he might also enjoy some ready cash from the proceeds. But not a dollar could he sell. He appealed to his associate who was finding a ready market for his stock, requesting the associate to help him dispose of his stock. But the associate refused, suggesting that "he do his own selling." This refusal resulted in a serious disagreement between the two men, which finally ended in a complete dissolution of their friendly business relations.

Now let us see what happens. The one who could not find a market for his stock was the fortunate one in the final crisis. The one with the ready initiative, who sold his stock, sold with it by so doing, his voice in the management of the business. When the climax was reached in their disagreement, the one who couldn't sell his stock naturally had, BY FORCE OF CIRCUMSTANCES, the control of the business, so he used his power to his own salvation and to the great detriment of his associate, by voting him out of the Presidency of the corporation and voting himself into that office.

The fact that he couldn't sell his stock was A BLESSING IN DISGUISE.

There was once a young man who was President of a corporation which was making lots of money. He owned automobiles, had servants and all the other luxuries which go with a successful business. He trusted his banker too far by borrowing money for expansion purposes. The banker wanted this young man's interest in the corporation, because he knew the young man was making lots of money and the banker happened to be dishonest. In the 1907 Roosevelt Panic he saw his chance and closed him out. It seemed like a dark day for the young man. All was lost. But watch the roulette wheel of destiny as it spins around by the force of the hand of fate. His loss forced him to go back to the practice of law. This brought him in touch with a million dollar corporation which employed him at a salary of $5,000.00 a year, a salary which he wouldn't have thought of accepting from an outsider while he was in control of his own business. This brought him to the middle west, and likewise in touch with the "big opportunity" of his life.

So his loss proved a blessing in disguise, for it literally drove him into a greater success.

A young bank clerk was discharged on account of his habit of drawing pictures of automobiles and sketching mechanical parts of automobiles during business hours. The loss of his job was quite a shock to him, for he supported his mother and two sisters from his small earnings as a bank clerk.

The loss of his bank job was the greatest blessing that ever came to him, for six months later he invented an automobile part which made him a fortune. He is now president of the largest automobile accessories companies in America. His clerks are all supplied with desk pads and pencils, with instructions to do all the drawing of automobiles they wish, and to submit to him any new ideas for improvements of automobile parts. Any of their ideas which he uses are paid for extra, at one hundred dollars each.

John D. Rockefeller discharged one of his faithful employees who he thought went too far in the exercise of his authorized duties, in making a financial transaction for Mr. Rockefeller in his absence, even though the deal netted Mr. Rockefeller several thousand dollars in cash.

A blessing in disguise. This office clerk, who had been honest and faithful, but not overly well paid, was immediately employed by one of Mr. Rockefeller's rivals, at a handsome salary. He now holds a high official position with the rival company.

And, while I write, further evidence of the soundness of my theory that "Adversity is usually a blessing in disguise" reaches me. One of the men mentioned in the beginning of this narrative — the one who was successful in selling stock, but who thereby lost the presidency of his company — has been elected president of a ten million dollar corporation, with an excellent chance to make $50,000.00 a year from his salary and dividends on his bonus stock in the company.

The ten million dollar corporation never would have been organized in all probability, except for the fact that this man's business associate supplanted him in his original position.

A blessing in disguise, for the ten million dollar corporation has patents and secret processes for making fuel, heat and light which probably will make this man immensely wealthy.

Every change in one's environment is for a purpose. That which seems like disappointment and ill "luck" usually is a blessing in disguise. If we do not carefully study cause and effect in all that we do and all that comes our way, we may never discover when and where our apparent failures are, in reality, blessings instead.

Stop and take an inventory of your life's record and see if you cannot find evidence in your own case which will support the correctness of this. Take an inventory of the lives of those you know intimately and see if the same is not true.

Then, when you become discouraged; when the

hand of fate seems to be against you; when your destiny seems doubtful and life's pathway fraught with many thorns of disappointment; when the rough and rugged hand of time spins the roulette wheel of fate so hard that the little pointer goes past your number just remember, friends, that there is a bigger stake awaiting you, if not in your present environment, then later on in some other "game" in the sphere of human accomplishments.

Hang on!

\* \* \*

## An English-Spanish Technical Journal devoted to Sugar Production.

Established 1899 — NEW YORK, N. Y., JANUARY, 1920 — Volume 22, No. 1

### France

The American sugar industry hardly realizes in what a pitiable condition the French industry is at this time. Stories to the effect that only fifty-one factories have been operating during the past season do not seem to convey a true conception of the situation as it actually exists. But when it is stated that, for instance, in 1901/2 the production of refined sugar was 1,082,000 metric tons, in 1912/13 877,600 tons, and in 1918/19 only 110,000 tons, or almost exactly 10 per cent of the 1902 production, then we begin to realize what the war has done to the French beet sugar industry.

One hundred and fifty sugar factories in France are either in ruins or their machinery has been depleted to such an extent as to make active working in the next two years out of the question. In addition, the fields have been showered with a rain of shells, many of which failed to explode and buried themselves deep in the ground, invisible to the eye of the tiller of the soil.

Last spring several beet sugar factories made attempts to arrange with their farmers to raise a new crop of beets on the shell-destroyed area. A number of deplorable accidents resulted when the plows struck the unexploded shells and blew the farmer with his team to pieces. Now an order has gone out that no more plowing or tilling is to take place on the former battlefields until the military authorities have gone over the ground foot by foot with delicate magnetic instruments, mounted on rubber-tired wheels, which will indicate the position of shells buried under-

# Self-Control

From **Sugar**, an English-Spanish technical journal devoted to sugar production, 1920

---

You can never become a great leader nor a person of influence in the cause of justice until you have developed great self-control.

Before you can be of great service to your fellowmen in any capacity you must master the common human tendency of anger, intolerance and cynicism.

When you permit another person to make you angry you are allowing that person to dominate you and drag you down to his level.

To develop self-control you must make liberal and systematic use of the Golden Rule philosophy; you must acquire the habit of forgiving those who annoy and arouse you to anger.

Intolerance and selfishness make very poor bed-fellows for self-control. These qualities always clash when you try to house them together. One or the other must get out.

The first thing the shrewd lawyer usually does when he starts to cross-examine a witness is to make the witness angry and thereby cause him to lose his self-control.

Anger is a state of insanity!

The well-balanced person is a person who is slow at anger and who always remains cool and calculating in his procedure. He remains calm and deliberate under all conditions.

Such a person can succeed in all legitimate undertakings! To master conditions you must first master self! A person who exercises great self-control never slanders his neighbor. His tendency is to build up and not to tear down. Are you a person of self-control? If not, why do you not develop this great virtue?

\* \* \*

# THE GLOVERS REVIEW

JAMES WARBASSE ESTATE  
PUBLISHERS

BETHUNE M. GRANT, JR.  
EDITOR

A GLOVE PERIODICAL FOR GLOVE PEOPLE

Published Monthly at Gloversville, New York

Subscriptions: $1.00 Yearly in the United States and Possessions—$1.50 Elsewhere—One Copy, Ten Cents

Entered as Second Class Matter at the Post Office at Gloversville, N. Y., under the Act of October 3, 1917

VOL. 21        JANUARY 1921        No. 1

THE New Year is opening with the country in one of the most trying phases of the reconstruction period. There have been, and still are, too many interests operating from antagonistic standpoints to permit of basic harmony. There is practically no stable price for anything, because, aside from articles of food and similar necessities, there is no market for anything. Merchants are buying from hand to mouth and in many instances are not even placing fill-in orders. The policy of retailers in general is to reduce stocks to the lowest point.

Everybody appears to be waiting until they are sure prices have reached rock bottom before they make a move. The theory back of this is plausible, but impracticable. If carried to its logical extreme it will result in the destruction of all business.

Mechanics understand that in order to obtain perfect balance they must, in theory at least, go back to the dead center, that infinitesimal point at the center of a revolving shaft or wheel which absolutely does not move. The human eye is not sufficiently refined to detect this dead center, yet it is an admitted, scientific fact.

Business is motion, visible motion at that. If business waits for the dead center of rock bottom prices to manifest itself, there will be no business left to perceive it. Business activity is often better than what would appear to be business certainty. A great American once expressed the opinion that the only man who never made a mistake was the man who never tried to do anything. He might well have added that such a man made the greatest mistake a man could make. A leading financier said that he was content if fifty-one percent. of his ventures proved profitable, because that left a balance in his favor. If either were alive today he would advise business to operate, even though it looked like taking a chance. Business is always more or less of a chance. That is why it appeals to the man with sporting blood in his veins. Business will have to take a lot of chances before it is again upon a stable foundation. Yet business men are anxious to get rid of all speculative features. Most of them are now more concerned to bring about stability than to pile up large profits. But they do not see how inactivity and depression can bring either profits or stability.

What the country needs today is to get the wheels of industry turning and keep them moving. Why cannot producers and distributors unite to bring this about? The longer unemployment continues the worse conditions will grow. The present non-buying policy of merchants is cutting off the source of their own prosperity. The purchasing power of the mass of consumers arises from their weekly wages. If merchants do not buy goods the factories cannot run and consumers will have no money with which to make purchases. It is a wheel within a wheel. If the inner wheel stops, the outer one must stop also. Wage earners cannot patronize stores unless they have money to spend. They can only procure money by earning wages. They are only paid wages when they work. Their employers can only give them work when merchants in their turn give employers orders.

Nobody blames merchants for acting guardedly. Merchants have lost money. So have manufacturers. It is not a question of what each has lost, but a question of getting together on a basis which will prevent further losses.

Manufacturers in many lines are offering goods at practically factory costs. They are doing this to keep their plants in operation and give their employes work. Their motive is sincere. They desire to meet merchants at some point of mutual understanding that will start the wheels moving. Will the merchants do their part?

Except for the gold standard of money, there is no absolute standard of value upon which and from which all other values can be reckoned. Mark Twain tells the story of an Esquimaux maiden who boasted to him that her father was the richest man of his tribe because he owned twenty-two iron fish hooks, while other members of the tribe had only bone fish hooks. That established iron fish hooks as the standard of wealth inside the Arctic circle.

Nobody knows what prices for any goods will be at the end of the year. It is argued that prices have not all dropped in equal ratio. They cannot yet, because there is no absolute standard by which to fix the equal and just relativity of prices. Even iron fish hooks will not do it. The ratio of prices will have to be worked out and it may take months, possibly years to do it.

Business men now realize that recovery is almost certain to be gradual. We have slowed down too much to get going at full speed all at once. Maybe it would be the worst thing that could happen if we did. But conservative, reliable, far seeing, cool headed and straight thinking business men believe that it is time to make a start.

Will the merchant and manufacturer co-operate to start things?

# A Definite Aim in Life

From **The Glovers Review**, January 1921

---

Careful analysis of more than 10,000 people disclosed a remarkable weakness which 95 per cent of them had in common — they had no definite aim in life!

Another notable fact disclosed by these ten thousand analyses was that those who were financially successful had a definite aim and a well formulated plan for achieving it.

As far as this writer has ever been able to ascertain, there are two steps which every successful person must take: first, he must formulate a very definite aim as an objective for which to strive, and secondly, he must reduce that aim to a concrete plan.

If you wish to witness a miracle which will equal anything that happened during biblical days, write out on paper a clear, concise statement of your aim in life, then memorize that which you have written.

Each night, just before you go to sleep; repeat your definite aim aloud several times, then, during the day, do everything within your power to further the achievement of that aim. In a short time the forces of the whole universe will seem to conspire to the end that you may realize your aim. Try it, doubting brother, try it.

\* \* \*

# LEATHER WORKER'S JOURNAL

Published Bi-Monthly by the United Leather Workers' International Union, Postal Bldg., Kansas City, Mo. Entered at Kansas City, Mo., post-office as second class mail matter.
Acceptance for mailing at special rate of postage provided for in Section 1103, Act of October 3, 1917, authorized July 15, 1918.

VOL. V—No. 1.        KANSAS CITY, MO., NOVEMBER, 1921.        $1.00 Per Year

## The Conspiracy Against Labor

The labor problem in its larger aspect as the problem of poverty is one of the persistent problems of the ages. It originated very early at the dawn of history and has run through the ages like the proverbial red thread. At times it has assumed an acute character and brought society to the verge of utter destruction. The worst phase it ever took on was when labor was degraded to the status of slavery. In some form or other, labor has always been an object of exploitation, possibly with the exception of the Christian Middle Ages, when it was enthroned in its proper place and when it received high honor and ample protection. At present, the old problem has cropped out with renewed virulence. It bristles with difficulties, as perhaps never before, and is fraught with terrible possibilities of evil.

In recent times the treatment of labor has been one that swings from extreme to extreme. We have seen labor petted and humored and in every way deferred to. If after such an experience, it acts as a spoiled child that should not be cause for surprise. But the pendulum already has swung to the other extreme. The blessings so fervently pronounced on labor have changed into equally fervent imprecations; the praises lavishly heaped upon it have turned into severe rebukes and bitter indictments. Just at present, labor is blamed for many things for which, if it is not entirely innocent of them, it shares the responsibility with others. It is taken to task most severely for its unwillingness to aid in the readjustment of the nation's industry by concurring heartily in the reduction of its wages. It is blamed for what is called ill-timed insistence on the closed shop, the labor union and collective bargaining. The sympathies of large sections of the people are being alienated from the cause of labor, as the result of this agitation. On the strength of this veering of public opinion, capital is beginning a new war on labor and trying to bring it back to a condition of tractableness and submission, which in the eyes of many is the only proper place for the workingman.

The worst thing for a child are parents that follow no fixed policy in education, but that allow themselves to be inspired by their moods which change from day to day and even from hour to·hour. It is precisely this attitude and policy, full of uncertainty, that generally prevails in the treatment of labor. Such treatment is not wholesome. It creates false expectations and arouses resentment.

Rarely does the public get the truth concerning labor troubles. They are mostly seen as through glasses, out of focus and grotesquely distorted. This for example is eminently true in the Virginia mine difficulties. The public has been treated to one side of the question, which of course is unfavorable to labor. The violence of labor has come in for round condemnation. But

# Achievement is Born of Sacrifice

From **Leather Worker's Journal**, November 1921

There can be no great achievement without a corresponding sacrifice. Christ gave his life that his philosophy might be planted in the human heart forever.

Think of one person, if you can, who has risen to fame or rendered the world a lasting service without sacrifice. Usually the value of the service rendered is in proportion to the sacrifice out of which it sprung.

Nature does not appear to favor the perpetuation of ideas or ideals which are not born of sacrifices and nurtured amid hardship and struggle. From the lowest mineral substance to the highest form of animal organism Nature gives evidence aplenty of her favoritism for that which is born of hardship, resistance and struggle.

The hardiest and finest trees of the forest are those which grew slowly and overcame the greatest resistance. No hothouse vegetable can equal those that are grown in the open, in opposition to the elements of the weather.

In a practical, material world of business, finance and industry we see evidence on every hand of the soundness of this philosophy.

Successes that are achieved overnight seldom endure. The greatest achievements in business are those which began at the very bottom, were based upon sound fundamentals and experienced seemingly impossible sacrifice. Before we envy Henry Ford his success we should meditate upon the struggles and hardships which he survived before he created the first Ford automobile. All of us would enjoy his great wealth but few of us would be willing to pay for it in sacrifice, as he has done.

If you are taking your baptism of fire and paying the price of sacrifice with faith in your handiwork, no matter what station in life you are striving to achieve you are apt to realize it if you carry on without losing faith, without turning back, without losing confidence in yourself and in the fundamental principle which insures achievement that corresponds to the nature and extent of your sacrifice.

\* \* \*

# The Seventeen Principles of Success

by Napoleon Hill

### 1) Definiteness of purpose

Definiteness of purpose is the starting point of all achievement. Without a purpose and a plan, people drift aimlessly through life.

### 2) Mastermind alliance

The Mastermind principle consists of an alliance of two or more minds working in perfect harmony for the attainment of a common definite objective. Success does not come without the cooperation of others.

### 3) Applied faith

Faith is a state of mind through which your aims, desires, plans and purposes may be translated into their physical or financial equivalent.

### 4) Going the extra mile

Going the extra mile is the action of rendering more and better service than that for which you are presently paid. When you go the extra mile, the Law of Compensation comes into play.

### 5) Pleasing personality

Personality is the sum total of one's mental, spiritual and physical traits and habits that distinguish one from all others. It is the factor that determines whether one is liked or disliked by others.

### 6) Personal initiative

Personal initiative is the power that inspires the completion of that which one begins. It is the power that starts all action. No person is free until he learns to do his own thinking and gains the courage to act on his own.

### 7) Positive mental attitude

Positive mental attitude is the right mental attitude in all circumstances. Success attracts more success while failure attracts more failure.

### 8) Enthusiasm

Enthusiasm is faith in action. It is the intense emotion known as burning desire. It comes from within, although it radiates outwardly in the expression of one's voice and countenance.

### 9) Self-discipline

Self-discipline begins with the mastery of thought. If you do not control your thoughts, you cannot control your needs. Self-discipline calls for a balancing of the emotions of your heart with the reasoning faculty of your head.

### 10) Accurate thinking

The power of thought is the most dangerous or the most beneficial power available to man, depending on how it is used.

### 11) Controlled attention

Controlled attention leads to mastery in any type of human endeavor, because it enables one to focus the powers of his mind upon the attainment of a definite objective and to keep it so directed at will.

### 12) Teamwork

Teamwork is harmonious cooperation that is willing, voluntary and free. Whenever the spirit of teamwork is the dominating influence in business or industry, success is inevitable. Harmonious cooperation is a priceless asset that you can acquire in proportion to your giving.

### 13) Adversity and defeat

Individual success usually is in exact proportion of the scope of the defeat the individual has experienced and mastered. Many so-called failures represent only a temporary defeat that may prove to be a blessing in disguise.

### 14) Creative vision

Creative vision is developed by the free and fearless use of one's imagination. It is not a miraculous quality with which one is gifted or is not gifted at birth.

### 15) Health

Sound health begins with a sound health consciousness, just as financial success begins with a prosperity consciousness.

### 16) Budgeting time and money

Time and money are precious resources, and few people striving for success ever believe they possess either one in excess.

### 17) Habits

Developing and establishing positive habits leads to peace of mind, health and financial security. You are where you are because of your established habits and thoughts and deeds.

# More titles from A Distant Mirror

**My Inventions**
Nikola Tesla

The autobiography by Nikola Tesla, first published in the magazine *Electrical Experimenter* in 1919. This new version has been re-edited, and has had illustrations added.

**The Problem of Increasing Human Energy**
Nikola Tesla

This book contains Tesla's thoughts on humanity's relationship with the universe, and also his explanation of the technological advancements embodied in his work. This text, first published in *Century Illustrated* magazine in June 1900, is yet another example of the genius of Nikola Tesla. New edition.

**Reconstruction by Way of the Soil**
Guy Wrench

"Our agriculture is wrongly based. It is a system largely directed at curing evils which it itself is responsible for. It is the wisdom of the country and the traditional farmers we need now; the wisdom of those who have built up long-lasting agriculture and whose wisdom lies in tradition."

**The Soul of the White Ant**
Eugene Marais

A passionate, insightful account into the world of termites. It is a meticulously researched expose of their complex, highly structured community life. Originally translated into English in 1937, the quality of research remains as relevant today as it was when it was first published. New edition.

A DISTANT MIRROR
*Publisher · Bendigo*
ADISTANTMIRROR.PRESS

www.ingramcontent.com/pod-product-compliance
Lightning Source LLC
Chambersburg PA
CBHW020707180526
45163CB00008B/2977